MANNERS IN THE LIBRARY

by Emma Bassier

Cody Koala

An Imprint of Pop!

popbooksonline.com

abdobooks.com
Published by Pop!, a division of ABDO, PO Box 398166, Minneapolis, Minnesota 55439.

Printed in the United States of America, North Mankato, Minnesota

102019
012020

THIS BOOK CONTAINS RECYCLED MATERIALS

Cover Photo: iStockphoto
Interior Photos: iStockphoto, 1, 5 (top), 5 (bottom left), 5 (bottom right), 9, 14, 15, 16–17, 19 (top), 19 (bottom left), 19 (bottom right), 21 (bottom left), 21 (bottom right); Shutterstock Images, 6, 11, 13, 21 (top)

Editor: Brienna Rossiter
Series Designer: Jake Slavik

Library of Congress Control Number: 2019942776

Publisher's Cataloging-in-Publication Data
Names: Bassier, Emma, author.
Title: Manners in the library / by Emma Bassier
Description: Minneapolis, Minnesota : Pop!, 2020 | Series: Manners matter | Includes online resources and index.
Identifiers: ISBN 9781532165634 (lib. bdg.) | ISBN 9781644942963 (pbk.) | ISBN 9781532166952 (ebook)
Subjects: LCSH: Manners--Juvenile literature. | Polite behavior--Juvenile literature. | Libraries--Juvenile literature. | Social customs--Juvenile literature. | Libraries and students--Juvenile literature.
Classification: DDC 395.12--dc23

Hello! My name is

Cody Koala

Pop open this book and you'll find QR codes like this one, loaded with information, so you can learn even more!

Scan this code* and others like it while you read, or visit the website below to make this book pop.

popbooksonline.com/manners-in-the-library

*Scanning QR codes requires a web-enabled smart device with a QR code reader app and a camera.

Table of Contents

Chapter 1

Many Items

It's a busy day at the library. Many students are doing homework. A **librarian** helps them use computers. The students show good **manners** by taking turns.

Watch a video here!

Manners depend on where a person is. Each place has different rules. People come to the library to read and learn. The library's rules help these people share its items.

Many libraries don't allow food or drinks. Spills could damage the library's items.

Chapter 2

Sharing Space

Many people visit the library. They all share the objects inside. To be **polite**, people take turns using computers. They leave space for others at tables.

Learn more here!

People often come to the library to study or work. Loud noises can **distract** them. Visitors shouldn't yell in a library. Instead, they should whisper or talk quietly.

The United States has more than 116,000 libraries.

Chapter 3

Sharing Objects

When you visit, be careful with the library's items. Don't write or draw on them. And don't rip pages. Remember that others will use the items too.

Learn more here!

People can borrow many items. They use library cards to check them out. They take the items home to use.

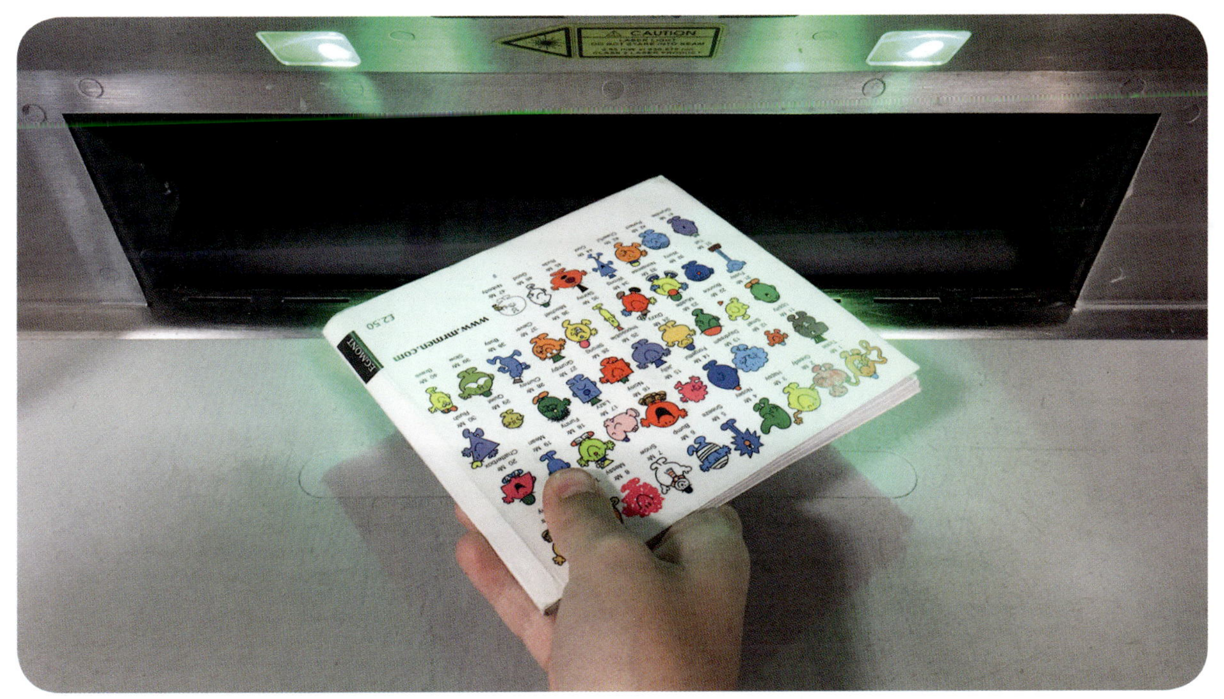

Then they bring them back by the **due date**.

People can check out books, movies, music, and much more.

People must take good care of the things they borrow. They must also return the

items on time. Someone else could be waiting to check the items out.

Chapter 4

Librarians

Librarians help people who come to the library. If a librarian is helping someone else, it is **polite** to wait. Do not **interrupt**. Instead, stand in line.

librarian

Complete an activity here!

Librarians make sure visitors follow the library's rules. Some rules limit how long people can use items. Other rules tell how to put items back in the correct spot. That way, other visitors can find and use them.

Share space with others.

Treat items with care.

Return items on time.

Making Connections

Text-to-Self

Have you ever been to a library? What kinds of items did it have inside?

Text-to-Text

Have you read other books about libraries? How were they similar to or different from this book?

Text-to-World

Many people use the books and computers at a library. What are other places where many people share the same things?

Glossary

distract – to take someone's attention away from what he or she is trying to focus on.

due date – the time something must be returned to the library.

interrupt – to start talking while someone else is still talking.

librarian – a person who works at a library.

manners – the correct words or actions for certain situations.

polite – showing good manners.

Index

Online Resources

popbooksonline.com

Thanks for reading this Cody Koala book!

Scan this code* and others like it in this book, or visit the website below to make this book pop!

popbooksonline.com/manners-in-the-library

*Scanning QR codes requires a web-enabled smart device with a QR code reader app and a camera.